Introduction To This C......

Hi folks.

I have been contacted by a number of people who wanted a print version of these two books. This is my first time using Amazon Create Space, and as I am having to reformat both ebooks, I figured I might as well offer combined edition ebook as well, at a slightly reduced price compared to purchasing both ebooks individually.

If you already purchased one or both, you might not care to purchase this version as well, and that is ok. I am not adding new content, beyond this intro section, and I made very minor changes in few versions of each ebook.

I removed duplicate content. For example, you would have had two same chapters regarding contact information, links to other books, and about series of books I titled "Path To Success".

I am hoping for the best here, but I am self publishing this, and things might not go as expected. Formatting for print book will be simplistic, and if that bothers you feel free to avoid it.

Jack Hunter

ABOUT "THE PATH TO SUCCESS"

Back in the Dark Ages before Internet, I wrote two books (really, ebooks, which amounted to lengthy text files in those days) that were popular with BBS (Bulletin Board Systems) crowd. Exact names I will leave out as times were different and while people books were intended for loved them, we live in time of too easily offended groups and I am not really certain that I would like any of my current work linked to them.

One book was about making money and it included chapters involving phreaking, hacking, white collar crime, and even had a chapter on how to make most money possible from a corpse while it's still fresh. It was de facto book on how to get money, and while I did not write it for profit originally, down the line we printed some copies (at school, so at no personal cost) and sold them to old fashioned mailing lists of folks who were buying books published by companies like the Paladin Press.

Second book was written because my friends kept asking for it. It was very basic treatise on how to pick up women, and how to psychologically work their defenses down to have sex within first few hours of you meeting them. This one also sold rather well.

As written, there is no chance whatsoever that any publisher would have been interested. They would simply offend far too many people. So while I refer to them as books, they originated as simple text files, and then they were printed on regular paper, bound primitively in cardboard binding with glue, and then stapled so they would not fall apart.

Fast forward, what seems like a couple of lifetimes, and here we are.

The Path of Success series of books are written as a spiritual successor to books that made me my initial capital. Times have changed. Original ideas are mostly pointless now as you do not need to do things like use a voice recorder to record coins dropping into a payphone to get free long distance, we all have cell phones and apps that give us free long distance anyway. You no longer need to mess with old fashioned advertisements, nor have 1-800 or 1-976 number, as people can simply email you, or chat live with you online. And even ways we pick up women changed in that overall morals are more relaxed now and casual sex is more of a norm. Number of methods I was recommending back then would just be not needed today, and could actually slow down your game rather than improve it.

While researching how best to present my new material, I read few hundred books on topics of making money and PUA. As far as PUA is concerned, I decided that I was only interested in filling in the blanks. You have thousands of self-promoting PUA artists rehashing same few points over and over. I can sum that up into 'just walk up to a girl and talk to her'. Yeah, these days it's that simple. You will get rejected by most, and eventually one will talk to you. No amount of books can adequately prepare you to talk to women face to face, it's something you need to go out there and do, repeatedly, a lot, to get good at. Things that I felt were not covered well were two topics, "How to Pick-Up Girls Online" and "How to

Pick Up Strippers". Most guys have very weak online game. And as I briefly owned a piece of a strip club (I wanted to be a DJ, nobody would let me, so I bought piece of a club and hired myself) I also had first-hand opportunity to see thousands of guys get used and abused by strippers and noticed average male has no clue how to deal with women who are professionals in exploiting their emotions. So I filled in the blanks with two books on that.

Making money online is a lot more complicated topic simply because majority of methods you might read about or buy information for will be outdated, used by too many other folks, and are mostly served to you by the people who cannot actually make money online in any way other than by selling you information which did not work for them.

You will see a lot of fake proofs of payment. You might see someone show you 1000 sales. What you do not see is that they bought those 1000 items on their own. Just like New York Times Best Seller book list is as corrupt as it gets with people hiring companies to buy their books and reviewers to write them glowing reviews. Want your book to make New York Times top 10? All you need is around 80 thousand dollars to buy your way onto it.

So how do you know who to trust?

I have no idea how to teach that. I learned through common sense and watching others fail and complain about it. I write for money. But, in all honesty, if money was all there is to it, I'd be writing Paranormal Romance for Amazon KDP because that is where real money for freelance and self-published authors is. I have no interest in romance whatsoever, maybe you guessed that by the fact that I go through more women than clean shirts. Money I like but what I like even more is showing off.

So, you can look at my main reason for writing this series of books as me demonstrating that I know more and can do better than almost anyone else out there doing exactly same things I do. My superiority complex is your gain, as you get to learn, fairly cheap, through right to the point, step by step, succinct, books, explaining precisely how things are really done.

I do not know how many of these books I will write. I do have about a dozen KDP pen names and in all honesty self-help is not exactly a money factory unless you want to promote yourself to an extreme. It's far easier to write cheap, gratifying, fiction.

I will begin with "How to Make Money Online" which should explain to any beginner how to make enough money to be able to afford rest of my books. Yeah, I am selfish and self-centered, I am only helping you make money so you can buy more of my books. Don't forget to buy dozen extra copies for friends and family.

One last thing to mention here is that I've noticed majority of people seem misguided about value of information and price in regards to quality of writing. They equate longer text with more value, which is simply insane way to look at it.

If you are looking for books where author is going to write in a manner where he takes thousand words to say something I can tell you using ten words, by all means just go find a different writer. I value time above all else as it is the only thing I cannot buy more of.

As a basic goal for each of these books I set to explain topic as best as possible in around 5000-10000 words. Then add pages that will go into every book, which might inflate final page and word count but are not core concept. That means that some of you will think 'this book is too short'. If that is something that will bother you, and you do not believe that my information is something you will wish to keep, Amazon has KDP program as a part of which they have cheap access to all the books you can read. I will include at least some of my books in it, and so you can just read it by borrowing it.

Do keep in mind that going rate for marketing ebooks explaining concepts which I am explaining, and I must say they generally do not come even close to quality of my writing, is $7-$37 for 8-20 page ebook. Majority of books in similar price range as this one will also just be written with intent to get you to buy more expensive product, also known as upsell. I do not do that. What you see is exactly what you are getting.

At the end of each book I will provide you with email through which you can email me suggestions. I do not guarantee that you will receive a reply, but odds are that if your suggestion was good it will be implemented.

LEGAL

In a perfect world there would be no need for Copyright and Legal sections. But we do not live in a perfect world. We live in a world where incompetent members of society love to lay blame on everybody but themselves as to why they suck at life. As I am writing this book to try to help those who are willing to try to help themselves, it is inevitable that it will get read by people who will try to follow what I advise and fail. Some will take that well, others might not. To protect myself legally from the latter I include this section in literally any book even remotely discussing any finances I write, although it probably does not need to be here. Please use common sense.

Earnings Disclaimer

This book is presented to you for information purposes only and is not a substitution for any professional advice. The contents herein are based on views and opinions of author and all associated contributors.

While every effort has been made by the author and all associated contributors to present accurate and up to date information within this document, it is apparent technologies rapidly change. Therefore, the author and all associated contributors reserve the right to update the contents and information provided herein as these changes progress. The author and/or all associated contributors take no responsibility for any errors or omissions if such discrepancies exist within this document.

The author and all other contributors accept no responsibility for any consequential actions taken, whether monetary, legal, or otherwise, by any and all readers of the materials provided. It is the reader's sole responsibility to seek professional advice before taking any action on their part.

Reader's results will vary based on their skill level and individual perception of contents herein, and thus no guarantees, monetarily or otherwise, can be made accurately. Therefore, no guarantees are made.

Affiliate Disclaimer

I may be an affiliate for products that I recommend. I do not recommend anything which I have not tried and trust personally. Or sometimes I might use affiliate links that belong to my friends or business associates in case of services that I know and trust, but do not currently hold personal nor business affiliate account for. I just do not like leaving money on the table, even if it's not for me, so whenever possible I try to give affiliate link so somebody gets something extra, including you.

If you purchase those items and/or services through my links I (or my friend/business/business associate) might earn a commission. Not always. Sometimes requirements might be that you need to actually buy right away and it gets more complicated from there depending on length of time cookie for that program works, and whether they go with first affiliate or last affiliate who receives reward. You will not pay more when buying a product through my link. In fact, I oftentimes am able to negotiate a lower rate (or bonuses) not available elsewhere for both you and me. So, if you want guarantee that my link is one that will be rewarded and that you will receive my version of the offer, clear your cookies/cache in your browser, close and reopen it and then click on my link. Or don't. Up to you.

HOW TO PICK UP STRIPPERS

THE PATH TO SUCCESS BOOK 3

JACK HUNTER

The Table of Contents is located on the last page of this book, for obvious reason.

COPYRIGHT

HOW TO PICK UP STRIPPERS © 2015 Jack Hunter

The Path to Success Book 3

3rd Electronic Edition

All Rights Reserved. No part of this publication may be reproduced, stored in a retrieval system, or transmitted, in any form or in any means – by electronic, mechanical, photocopying, recording or otherwise – without prior written permission.

Having stated the above, if you obtained this book through piracy, I hope that you read it, understand it and that it helps you.

Poor people are poor because they are stupid and ignorant. If what I wrote helps you move up socially and financially, great. I am not against piracy as I find that majority of people on this planet cannot easily afford price of a book like this one, although it is cheaper than just one Starbucks coffee where I live. I volunteered in a number of 3rd world countries and I realize that in some places this is more than a person could scrounge together. In Sierra Leone most people make just 3 American Cents per hour. However, if my books do help you, and you do make money, I will ask you to remember to come back, purchase a legitimate copy and leave feedback to let others know that it might help them as well.

I am against DRM (Digital Rights Management) and my ebooks do not use it.

Enjoy.

LEGAL

In a perfect world there would be no need for Copyright and Legal sections. But we do not live in a perfect world. We live in a world where incompetent members of society love to lay blame on everybody but themselves as to why they suck at life. As I am writing this book to try to help those who are willing to try to help themselves, it is inevitable that it will get read by people who will try to follow what I advise and fail. Some will take that well, others might not. To protect myself legally from the latter I include this section in literally any book even remotely discussing any finances I write, although it probably does not need to be here. Please use common sense.

Earnings Disclaimer

This book is presented to you for information purposes only and is not a substitution for any professional advice. The contents herein are based on views and opinions of author and all associated contributors.

While every effort has been made by the author and all associated contributors to present accurate and up to date information within this document, it is apparent technologies rapidly change. Therefore, the author and all associated contributors reserve the right to update the contents and information provided herein as these changes progress. The author and/or all associated contributors take no responsibility for any errors or omissions if such discrepancies exist within this document.

The author and all other contributors accept no responsibility for any consequential actions taken, whether monetary, legal, or otherwise, by any and all readers of the materials provided. It is the reader's sole responsibility to seek professional advice before taking any action on their part.

Reader's results will vary based on their skill level and individual perception of contents herein, and thus no guarantees, monetarily or otherwise, can be made accurately. Therefore, no guarantees are made.

Affiliate Disclaimer

I may be an affiliate for products that I recommend. I do not recommend anything which I have not tried and trust personally. Or sometimes I might use affiliate links that belong to my friends or business associates in case of services that I know and trust, but do not currently hold personal nor business affiliate account for. I just do not like leaving money on the table, even if it's not for me, so whenever possible I try to give affiliate link so somebody gets something extra, including you.

If you purchase those items and/or services through my links I (or my friend/business/business associate) might earn a commission. Not always. Sometimes requirements might be that you need to actually buy right away and it gets more complicated from there depending on length of time cookie for that program works, and whether they go with first affiliate or last affiliate who receives reward. You will not pay more when buying a product through my link. In fact, I oftentimes am able to negotiate a lower rate (or bonuses) not available elsewhere for both you and me. So, if you want guarantee that my link is one that will be rewarded and that you will receive my version of the offer, clear your cookies/cache in your browser, close and reopen it and then click on my link. Or don't. Up to you.

INTRODUCTION

About Jack Hunter

I am not going to write in third person. Every time I read those about sections and they state "author is blah, blah" and we all know its author himself/herself who wrote it, it just looks weird. Nor do I feel like writing an autobiography here. Quite frankly, who I am is irrelevant. What I know and can share with you is why we are here. I'll also skip pictures of earnings as 'proof' as that sort of thing is nonsense that only works on weak minded, and I'd like to think that caliber of person choosing to read what I write is bit better than that. We all know all those proofs of earning are mostly just fake anyway.

English is not my first, nor second, nor … well I might have started learning it as a third or fourth or fifth. I do not remember. I went through lots of languages, and I tend to use at least three every single day. So normally I'd need an editor to ensure that my writing looks professional when it's something this size. I am not using one and we will see how that goes. It should be fine except that I sometimes skip using articles like 'the', 'a' and 'an' as they do not exist in most languages.

About This Book

Objective of this book is to teach you how to pick up a stripper and get laid. Ideally for free, but unless you see and speak to a stripper outside by the door odds are that you will be out at least cash for one overpriced drink.

Objective is not to get anyone to like you, or to date you. Just to get laid, as fast as possible, with, in this books case, a stripper.

There are other books on picking up strippers out there. I've read few and my problem with them is that it's fairly obvious that those books are not written by guys who really pick up strippers for free, but by guys who end up giving strippers money. And if you pay for her, then your game really does not matter, she would do you for cash no matter what you look like and no matter what you say.

I had a small investment in strip club in Montreal, Quebec, Canada, and I worked while owning piece of it as a strip club DJ. For just over three years. I've dated several strippers, I've slept with few dozen strippers, and while I was making lot more money than they did, it's them who paid for things for me, from buying me food and paying for my drinks and party favors, to paying for hotel rooms, driving me around, and variety of gifts.

All strippers want to quit stripping. They all want to meet a nice guy who will rescue them and give them safe life. Problem is that they are very delusional and unrealistic. Most of them have children. They might have husband, boyfriend, or both. They have variety of sugar daddies. And longer a woman is a stripper more chance that she is also a seasoned prostitute and unable to really care about a guy.

They expect guys to not be jealous. Should you become actual boyfriend of one, and I've met many beta type guys who did, you can expect to have to take care of her children and play second fiddle to anything else she wants. Understand, she is used to guys treating her like she is a 10, even if she is a 5.

So however you choose to use information I provide, I will suggest that you stick to just sleeping with whatever you pick up short term. Do not make any long term plans, no matter how sweet she might seem. They become very good at pretending. And in my experience they also fail to consider anything they do cheating. Do not be stupid, use condoms.

And, a smart man once said that a book should only be as long as it needs to be. I write books that can be read in one sitting and that will improve your life. If you want to read a novel, this is not it. What this is, is a simplest way for anyone to go get laid with a stripper, right now. It's written to be short, simple and to the point. This is NOT meant to be all-encompassing at all, nor is it a tutorial. It points you in the right direction with assumption that you are intelligent enough.

HOW MUCH IS THIS GOING TO COST ME?

That is an excellent question. Strip clubs are designed to get you to spend all of your money, no matter how much you have. Just like casinos. Guy at front door you see first, we called them 'hawkers', guy that's yelling "Come in, we have beautiful girls", or something bit more racy than that, is first one that will hit you up for cash. He will usually ask you for something between five and twenty dollars. I suggest not entering any place where "I do not want to pay any cover" fails to get you in. Any place where they will insist is probably constantly busy and it bad for pick up. So do NOT pay cover.

After you are in, there might be a coat check. They might claim that it's mandatory. Do not pay for that either. And if you do give them you jacket or backpack count on possibility of it being stolen. So, do not bring anything you'd need to check, and if you are wearing a jacket, insist that your previous experience resulted in stolen jacket, refuse to check it and keep it with you inside.

Then there might be second guy inside, usually built like a football linebacker, who will try to take you to "your seat". Refuse that as well. All he wants is more money from you for nothing.

If you were an idiot, you might be out as much as 50 dollars before you even order your first drink.

After you sit, and I suggest sitting at the bar at first, they might have two drink minimum. If regular beer, say Budweiser, is $3-$5 at a local bar, strip club will charge you $10 per beer + tip. You do not want to get drunk, and you want to drink whatever you ordered very slowly. Most intelligent thing to do is not to drink alcohol in strip club at all, just pay $5 per glass for Cola or juice and sip it slowly. You are here to get laid. Nothing else. And you might have to hit several strip clubs in a row to score.

Depending on where strip club is located physically and local laws those strippers might have to keep panties on, and dances might be contact or non-contact. If it's no contact, she can place her hands on you and touch you (not overtly sexually), if its full contact you are allowed to run your hands along her body, grab her breasts, but are not allowed to touch her vagina. If unsure, ask the girl, the bartender or DJ. Bouncers are usually dumbest, but most threatening guys they can find, and they usually are clueless. Plus at most clubs bouncer is job with highest turnaround, they constantly get fired and replaced. Sometimes it's because they have that job because they are boyfriend of one of girls and as soon as they fight, it's he that loses job, as club needs girl more.

Dances can also be separated into table dance (she dances at your table, everyone can see her) and booth dances (sometimes private room dances, but rarely).

Dances will run you $10-$30 per 3 minutes. However you are there to pick her up, for free. If you take girl for a dance, you become a customer and you can say bye bye to chance to screw her for free. She will be unable to stop seeing you as her ATM.

Those are all associated costs, unless you might need a hotel room after pickup, in which case tack on $40-$60 for a room. If there are by the hour motels available, then it can be as low as $20.

WHAT TO WEAR?

It does not matter. Yet it does.

I know all the 'guru's will tell you to wear expensive clothing and to play up the 'I'm so important' part. In my experience, wealthier you look, harder it will be to get her to buy you things. And I always, always, always want girls to pay for everything. I used to dress up and I kept running into gold diggers far too often. Not only in strip clubs, but in general. And gold diggers tend not to put out fast because they want wealthy guy to think they are a nice girl. Which is just nonsense if all you want is to get laid.

So I find that 'party boy' look, or wearing things like cargo pants that look bit work out, simple plain t-shirt, or a plain hoodie (plain because if you have anything on it, people judge you, and I try to be tabula rasa, clean slate, I do not want them to know anything about me at all), works best. Or track pants, sneakers.

You can seriously wear whatever you normally would wear. You just adjust your game slightly if you insist that she have preconceived notions about you. Most PUA guys try to peacock. I try to do the opposite. To just blend in. That way, like a ninja, I always surprise them. They never know what exactly to expect. And it's always far easier to pick up a girl who is not expecting you to be picking her up and so has her guard down.

Another thing to understand is that when you peacock, you might be singled out to be assaulted by drunks or guys who are striking out with girl you are talking to, angry and drunk. Since my methods mostly involve hitting places I've never been before, and blending in so if I am striking out with a girl, rest do not take notice, which would be a bad thing.

Think about it. If you have 12 inch red/green Mohawk and are wearing Technicolor Raincoat, you might be the guy on whom all eyes will go to. If you try to put moves on one girl, and fail, everybody in that entire place noticed. If you wear jeans, sneakers and plain t-shirt, and you learn how to test girls quietly, you might get to take all numbers of all girls you are interested in, in entire place, without any of them thinking you hit on anyone else.

Obviously if you intend to go to a place where all guys wear suits, you'd wear a similar suit, but I hit places where I'll get 18 year old University girls so I look the part.

WHEN TO GO?

Never on a Friday night. No matter what else you do, Fridays are the absolutely the worst day to waste your time picking up strippers. Even ugliest strippers will be busy Friday nights. I do not work the 9-5 type work, but most people do, and Friday nights in every city seem to be like New Year's Eve in New York Times Square.

On a Sunday and Monday majority of the better looking strippers will not be working.

Most wage slaves get paid on a Thursday or Friday.

So you want to go Tuesdays and Wednesdays.

Best time of the month is right after 1st of the month. You want most other guys to be low on cash on day you go out. People usually pay bills around 1st and cheque that they receive right around 1st is one that rent and most major bills get paid from.

Best time of the year is end of the summer. Late August if you want to be very specific. This is two decades of year round experience.

Thing is, your city might be slightly different, and exact best day and time will vary. So what you might want to do is hit the town once on each day, Monday through Sunday, in same week, one day after another. Around 9pm. And see how crowd in each strip club in your area is. Your ideal strip club will have very few guys, and decent looking girls at least some of whom still look very fresh and young.

Once you know what you are doing and can do all this quickly, best time to enter strip club is 15 minutes before last call. That is usually 75 minutes before strip club will close for the night.

HOW TO SELECT MS. RIGHT STRIPPER?

All strippers are messed up to an extent. So we don't really need to split them up into too many categories. Nearly all of them will be substance abusers, whether they are alcoholics or heroin addicts or just smoke marijuana non-stop. Nobody in their right mind can work a job like stripping and remain ok in the head for long.

So if you want anything more than just to get laid, you should strictly aim for ones that have been doing it less than couple months tops. If during a date she mentions that she was ever molested, raped, sexually abused in any way, or a prostitute, that is not a girl to plan a life with, no matter how desperate you are. I spent solid portion of my life as a psychiatrist and you cannot help those girls. You can medicate them. Forever.

If objective is just to get laid, easiest strippers to pick up are either newbies or ones who have done it too long and are looking for a guy to take them away. All the rest will be in money making mindset and it will be much harder to break them out of it.

Whoever you pick, in general, you need to make them think that it will be a relationship. That there is a possibility of a relationship. That you are a guy they have been waiting for. The right guy. Not an asshole like all the other guys she's ever been with.

Hottest stripper in the place will most likely know it and not be interested in you. That type generally require too much work unless you are a drug dealer or have access to whatever her drug of choice is. And then you are technically paying for her anyway.

Ugliest stripper in the place will know it too. And she might be easiest to score, but do you really want her?

Other than those two, you will have between maybe sex and eighteen other girls there to choose from, depending on the size of the place and the day and time.

Now, this part is very important.

You want her to know you are interested, but not too interested. You also do not want her to see you checking out other girls at all.

If she does not know you are interested, she might not talk to you. In strip clubs, girls are ones doing the picking up. Ok, unless you are a total loser and call her over and just pay.

If she knows you are very interested, again, you'll end up being looked at as ATM.

While outside of strip club, in regular PUA, your looks really do not matter, inside a strip club, they do. At least, they do matter if you want stripper without paying her.

So, you want to discreetly see each of girls there look at you, and judge how interested they are in you, based on how they look at you. You need to do this fairly quickly, and as soon as you get in.

Some girls might be in booths giving private dances when you come in, so if you want to see full inventory, you can buy yourself some time by looking busy, like checking text messages or something, in which case they will skip you at first.

Once girl you want approaches your table, it's too late for anything else, the game is on.

HOW TO PICK UP A STRIPPER?

This is part all those gurus tend to get 100% wrong every time.

Out in the street or in regular bar where girls are drunk and will do any guy if drunk enough, for free, cockiness works. But, in the strip club, all the assholes are always cocky. They come in, act like douchebags, try to touch girls without paying, waste girl's time. Remember, I had an inside job, as a DJ. Girls would come talk to me about what they do not like.

You need to be alone. You need to not be sitting near stage. And you can't act too interested and cocky because then you will be stereotyped which will work against you.

Although you are in a strip club, you can still get yourself friend zoned and lose all hope of ever sleeping with her.

That usually happens if she decides you are not going to be a customer, but that you are not boyfriend material either.

One way or the other she will know what she wants from you within few minutes, so you must be quick.

When she approaches your table, her goal is to get you to buy her overpriced drink from the bar, for which she will get paid her cut (they might give her just orange juice if she asks for a screwdriver, but charge you $10) and more importantly to get you to pay her for private dances until she takes all of your money.

Depending on strip club you are in, she might be prohibited from sitting with you if you do not buy her a drink. But you need to decide how interested she is before you pay for it. Longer you are talking to her more chance that she gets upset at you wasting her time, unless club is near closing and/or empty anyway, which is why all that "when to go" calculations we discussed earlier are important.

If you are feeling it and think she is the one, buy her one drink.

Your first objective is to get her to tell you her real name. I simply ask her directly. She might say "My name is Melody" and I'll say "I get that's your stage name, but I cannot take you seriously as a person while thinking of you only as your job. What is your real name?"

If she does not give you her real name forget it, she is not interested. If she does, you are halfway there. Seriously. Prostitutes of all kinds will not give their real name to clients. It's one of those 'rules' that I saw over and over again.

I work with minimal waste of my time. I value my time greatly. I am sure some guys can keep harassing one girl until she is drunk enough and they eventually break her down, but I am not into that, so my advice is to play numbers and be quick. Practice makes perfect and will result in you always getting a girl any night you want one.

If you walk over to hundred, thousand, million different girls and simply say "I want to have sex with you." eventually one will say ok. That would work on strippers as well, but with lower chance so the 'I am a great guy' routine simply works faster.

Avoid letting her lead. She has few lines she said millions of times to thousands of guys. She is comfortable in her salesman's pitch and you want to throw her off balance.

Do NOT, under ANY circumstances, say anything negative about her being a stripper. If at any point she thinks you are talking down to her, your game is over with her. Remember, this is a girl who all the other guys there constantly tell she is perfect. She might want guy to take her away, she might HATE stripping, but she wants guy who respects her. They get just as crazy about respect as feminists.

Do NOT criticize her.

If she says that she thinks she is too fat, you reply either that you like her exactly as she is, or that she is not as fat as she thinks she is. You do not say something like "you are fine", as she will take it badly.

If she has stretch marks from having kids, or a scar, and mentions it (if she does not, avert your eyes, do not stare) you can say "Oh, I did not even notice it until you mentioned it. Really, it's barely noticeable, and it does not detract from how sexy you look at all".

If she says that she is only stripping to get through university or college, you switch topic from stripping, where you'll mess up eventually, to "Oh, cool, what are you studying?" followed by, no matter what she is studying "That's great. I have a cousin who does that and I hear it's very rewarding/makes lot of money/whatever compliment."

Try to somehow toss into conversation that you dated a stripper. But probably you should use term 'dancer' instead, they all think they are performing art, like ballerinas. One of main issues strippers have with guys is that most guys cannot handle stripper girlfriend being groped by other guys. Same lines that work on porn stars and other types of prostitutes, work great on strippers.

Best line is "Love and sex are totally different. " It exemplifies lie all whores constantly tell themselves. Some save anal sex or kissing only for boyfriend/husband and think that elevates them from common whores. It does not, but if you want to have sex with them, you agree and make them feel like a born again virgin.

Simply steer conversation, quickly, from getting her real name, to asking her about herself, make her think you want to know her better and think she is special, and then just get her out of there asap. It's that simple. Do not overcomplicate things. Do not talk to her too long. Longer you talk, more you risk not getting laid with her.

Your goal to close this deal is to have her meet you outside the club. She will NOT be allowed to leave with you. You cannot make anything obvious, like giving her a number, or taking hers. But you can have her input it into your phone discreetly while pretending to look at something.

Alternatively you can ask her to meet you after place closes, or to cut her day short right away, and go wait for her someplace nearby which she suggests.

Not another bar.

I prefer to make it be something like all night coffee shop or decent food place, and to do this as close to 3am as possible when she would be leaving anyway. Sometimes she is willing to go with you, but has a kid, or boyfriend waiting at her place, and can only spare an hour or less.

So have motel ready nearby.

CONCLUSION

Ok, as I already mentioned, strippers are crazy. They are insane. Remember that.

That means that they might do things that make absolutely no sense to you whatsoever.

A stripper who seemed into you and agreed to meet you outside might get bouncer to escort her to a taxi and split without explanation. All the drugs she is doing might make her paranoid. She might be bi-polar, or some other kind of looney.

As I do not like to waste time, I might hit five clubs early on, like 9pm-11pm, and setup maybe three meets after 3am. Then text all of them right around 3am and ask if we are still on. You'd be surprised how many ignore your text, give you wrong number, or otherwise start to behave stupid after just four hours. If all three are fail, that gives me time to hit one or two more clubs and try for another one. If more than one still will show, I pick one I like best and reschedule others to either hour after or next day, quoting something like 'I'm surgeon and we have guy who got shot 15 times emergency. I have to go, I'm on call, but I really like you, so can we see each other bit later?'

Main key is to always have several girls in rotation, none of whom know your home address.

If you fail to take that bit of wisdom, then you get to deal with looney strippers slashing your tires, throwing bricks through your windows and posting on Facebook whatever they can creatively come up with that will make you look bad. Not to mention sleep with guys who look much more dangerous than you and try to get you beat up or killed. So, keep your home safe by keeping strippers away from it.

Plenty of gurus seem to just copy bad advice from each other and will tell you to go kiss ass of bouncers (worthless), managers (also worthless) and bartenders. Only bartenders might be useful. People get drunk, and amazingly enough always seem to talk to bartenders. Bartenders tend to talk about it to those they are friends with. Be that friend and you just might get something useful from it, like a good stock tip or be warned that stripper you are hitting on is dating bouncer who put last guy who was hitting on her in the hospital.

As ex DJ I can tell you that us DJ's are mostly self-absorbed when working. Meaning that while tons of people would tip me to play some song, while I'd play them their song, if you ask me to point them out of lineup week later, I just couldn't remember. And my memory is perfect, it's just pointless to pay attention to hundreds of guys who try to talk to you each day as most are drunk, obnoxious and want to talk about stripper they like and try to get info about her.

If stripper likes you, but she really needs money, she might mention it. At this point, I'd just get her number and not waste time there. If she goes to dance for someone else, she might forget about you. She might come back three hours later. Either way, you are not on her priority list and if you are seriously sitting there and waiting for her, I suggest you go read as much as you can about PUA and ideas of perceived value until its crystal clear why that's just stupid.

Finally, if you end up getting friend zoned by a stripper, you can still turn that to your advantage by getting her help to get laid by another stripper.

And if all else fails, or you really want one specific stripper, I've never seen one turn down money.

Funny way of doing that part is to ask her if she would make a porno film with you for ridiculous amount of money. Just tell her you are not famous but some relative or ex is, and Red Light District are offering you 500k, or a million and you'll split it with her.

She will say yes, then you lower her cut. Maybe to 100k, saying you have other expenses. She will be disappointed but she will still agree. Then you toy with her dropping amount, or just fast forward and say, "Ok, how about for $1". Here she will get upset and say whatever nonsense, and you can say something like "Well, I just want to be sure that we will play well together first, before I take you to the studio" and then you get her free or very cheap for 'casting shoot'. If you want, you can even have her sign release form and sell that homemade porn.

Remember, if she agrees to ANY amount, she is a whore. Everything else is just negotiating the price, even if in the end that price is free.

Alternative way is to tell her you are a modelling agent, which works better if you get some business cards made which say that on them. You can go with Playboy or Elle Magazine, or just make up a magazine. Then ask her for test shoot. Then tell her how shoots are $5000 but maybe you can make a deal, and get free sex.

Or same deal but you are casting scout for some big Hollywood firm.

You are dealing with women who failed at life, who have little to no education, low IQ, and who like easy money. Lying to them is easiest thing in the world. But I always felt that it lowers my achievement if I lie, so I always try everything else first.

Anyway, don't hate the player, hate the game.

Good luck and go get laid.

HOW TO PICK UP GIRLS ONLINE

THE PATH TO SUCCESS BOOK 4

JACK HUNTER

The Table of Contents is located on the last page of this book, for obvious reason.

COPYRIGHT

HOW TO PICK UP GIRLS ONLINE © 2015 Jack Hunter

The Path to Success Book 4

3rd Electronic Edition

All Rights Reserved. No part of this publication may be reproduced, stored in a retrieval system, or transmitted, in any form or in any means – by electronic, mechanical, photocopying, recording or otherwise – without prior written permission.

Having stated the above, if you obtained this book through piracy, I hope that you read it, understand it and that it helps you. Poor people are poor because they are stupid and ignorant. If what I wrote helps you move up socially and financially, great. I am not against piracy as I find that majority of people on this planet cannot easily afford price of a book like this one, although it is cheaper than just one Starbucks coffee where I live. I volunteered in a number of 3rd world countries and I realize that in some places this is more than a person could scrounge together. In Sierra Leone most people make just 3 American Cents per hour. However, if my books do help you, and you do make money, I will ask you to remember to come back, purchase a legitimate copy and leave feedback to let others know that it might help them as well.

I am against DRM (Digital Rights Management) and my ebooks do not use it.

Enjoy.

INTRODUCTION

About Jack Hunter

I am not going to write in third person. Every time I read those about sections and they state "author is blah, blah" and we all know its author himself/herself who wrote it, it just looks weird. Nor do I feel like writing an autobiography here. Quite frankly, who I am is irrelevant. What I know and can share with you is why we are here. I'll also skip pictures of earnings as 'proof' as that sort of thing is nonsense that only works on weak minded, and I'd like to think that caliber of person choosing to read what I write is bit better than that. We all know all those proofs of earning are mostly just fake anyway.

English is not my first, nor second, nor … well I might have started learning it as a third or fourth or fifth. I do not remember. I went through lots of languages, and I tend to use at least three every single day. So normally I'd need an editor to ensure that my writing looks professional when it's something this size. I am not using one and we will see how that goes. It should be fine except that I sometimes skip using articles like 'the', 'a' and 'an' as they do not exist in most languages.

About This Book

Picking up girl online demands entirely different game plan than picking up girl offline. Main difference is that online they get hit on a lot more. A girl who is a 5/10 and would get ignored offline will still get few dozen guys hitting on her online. A 9/10 who would be turning down dozens at a club will have literally, and I am not kidding nor exaggerating, thousands of guys hitting on her online each week.

If you've read any of my other books you should know by now that I am all about keeping things simple. Rather than write 200 page book full of worthless filler that you will waste your time trying to find good info in, my books are actionable info only. Short on fluff means easy to read in one sitting, easy to locate part you want to reread later, and easy to follow through on.

Should you choose to read this book you will know more about how online game works than most guys and that should give you a leg up on your competition.

This is NOT a guide on how to find a long term relationship. This is a guide on how to go online and get laid. Ideally within couple of hours. For free. With a girl you will find at least somewhat attractive.

It's written to be short, simple and to the point. This is NOT meant to be all-encompassing at all, nor is it a tutorial. It points you in the right direction with assumption that you are intelligent enough to research further whatever topics interested you.

FREE VS PAID

You can pick up girls on actual dating sites or you can do it in other online venues, like Facebook or Craigslist. Most of this book will concentrate on actual dating sites as what you learn from that can easily be adapted to work any other place online. Funny thing is, it is actually much harder to pick up a girl on a dating site where she supposedly wants to be picked up on, then on Facebook where she proclaims that she has a boyfriend or a husband and that she is not interested at all. Reason for that is that girls get hit on no matter where they go, but Facebook is where they are posting their own recent selfies and feel comfortable. If things do not go well, they have friends and family right there at the click of a button. It's almost like if they were at a family oriented house party.

Problem for you is that if you pick up girls openly on Facebook, when things go sour, and they always do, she will post your pictures and can start PMing your friends and family to tell them how bad of a person you are. Online version of a crazy girl keying your car or throwing brick through your window. It's also lot harder to stop online stalkers than offline ones.

So obvious choice is to stick to partial anonymity and use dating sites instead. Unless you never want to meet girls in person and you just want to talk about things with them rather than do things to them. Different strokes for different folks, you can use what I tell you either way, but I prefer the real thing.

Even if they advertise as free, dating sites exist to make money. That means that they will place some sort of roadblocks in your way to make your free experience less pleasant than if you pay.

My dating site experience is based on strictly two sites. Plenty of Fish and OK Cupid. And I do not believe in paying to get laid, actually I believe in getting girls to spend money on me, so obviously I just used them on free accounts.

Girls who pay dating site are desperate. They are not kind you want. Actually they are kind you want to skip. When a woman pays dating site it signals that she wants to get married, that she either wants to have children as soon as possible or that she is a single mother, very lonely, and that she needs a man. She might be in debt and unable to take care of herself. Whatever her issues, you do not want desperate.

I am all about path of least resistance. That means you want the fun girls instead. The easy girls. The slutty girls. It does not matter what you call them. The type of girls who are horny, who do want to get laid, who do put out on a first date, usually right away if you skip entire date nonsense and meet at your place or hers, and who sometimes do more than one guy.

So, you want to make free accounts only, and stick to girls who are also on free accounts. That lands you in the middle of the cesspool, the Wild West of online dating scene, but it's exactly where you will want to be to get laid easily.

LOWER EXPECTATIONS

Being good looking does help. But, it's not a necessity. Different girls are attracted to different things and while majority might be into muscular young guys, fact is that muscular young guys are not interested in majority of them. So they have to lower their expectations.

And, it's critical to understand that for online dating scene you too need to lower your expectations.

I am not saying that you need to have sex with ugly women, just that if you are used to 7's and 8's offline, you should get used to 5's and 6's online.

You can still land a 9 online but it is going to take ridiculous amount of effort in comparison. Unless you just pay them.

In my case, I did online pick up's just for fun. I prefer offline game by far. In your case, maybe you are too shy or less than average in looks and need to build your confidence to work your way up to offline game. And that is fine.

When you look at girls' profile picture you need to understand that it's most likely not what she looks like. Statistically it's most likely her picture but about five to ten years old. There is also a possibility that it's a picture of her better looking friend, especially if they always post pictures where they are surrounded by other girls and you never know which one you are really talking to. And there is also a possibility of picture not being her at all. Even if there are several pictures, it means nothing.

It might not even be a girl. It can be random homosexual, or ex who wants to humiliate girl in pictures, or one of her friends trying to get her a date without her even knowing about it.

Another possibility is that it is the girl and she did make that account, but it was two years ago and she is no longer logging in. Dating sites are notorious for leaving inactive profiles of pretty girls on indefinitely. Guys PM them, thinking those girls are there, PM's get auto-deleted and those profiles are just ghosts.

So name of online game is quantity over quality, to a much higher extent than offline game. You are not only playing numbers with girls themselves, but with all other nonsense.

Typical newbie mistake is to select only few profiles to PM and to do dumb things like read into their profiles too much, to stare at their pictures trying to see something. It's like that guy who follows around pretty girl who friendzoned him thinking that he will sleep with her. Not a chance. Except online you might not even be looking at actual girl at all.

TYPES OF GIRLS ON ONLINE DATING SITES

While average guys tend to find women complicated, they really are not. You can psychologically split them up to simplify how to play the game. This is a simplified list suitable for a beginner. As you go along you can decide to make your own categories as it helps to categorize women you are in some stage of game with. I don't know about you, but I talk to so many that I forget who is who and what do they want, unless I keep notes. Keep in mind that whole point here is just to meet them, get laid, and get out. Not to date any. But it helps if you know their motivations because then you can tell them what they really want to hear.

1. Transgender 'girl'. Yeah, I have to list this out there. It is not a real girl, to me, pre (has penis) or post (has man made vagina) op, but fact remains that these people do go on dating sites, and they list themselves as 'female'. Sometimes they are honest and write what they are in profile, but rather often they want to pretend that they are a real female. I do not really have much to say on them other than that it's usually obvious and that even if you are into

trannies, dating site ones will probably be far more trouble than you want.

2. BBW. The Fat Girl. The Land Beast. The Shamu. More cushion for the pushing. More of her to love. This is by far most common type of girl in North America. Fat. Obese. Huge. If you are a chubby chaser or just desperate enough you might be into this. They require little to no game on your part. Chances are that their self-esteem is already fairly low, much lower than that of average female. They might be a bitch outwardly, but that is just a self-defense mechanism in action as they are used to guys hurting them. Say something along lines of 'I care lot more about the mind than about the body' and they are in the bag.

3. Feminazi. Femape. OK Cupid has thousands of these. These are women that want just the good parts of being a female without any of the bad. They enjoy playing a victim. They will mention that they were raped at some point, even to total strangers, and often. Odds are that they were never actually raped, but they do

not want to be excluded. They believe in nonsense like 'rape culture', and 'patriarchy', and surround themselves with Beta males.

These women are really stupid. They are generally making decisions that equal to branding themselves low class and undesirable by any sane male because they lack foresight about future. You can expect them to have scars from self-harming (they literally tend to slice themselves), tattoos, to claim to be pansexual, piercings all over their body, and in more extreme cases they might refer to women as 'womyn' and seriously have hatred towards men, while claiming to just be 'modern, liberated women'.

Unless you are retarded and agree with their nonsense, to score a feminazi you have to lie.

Just toss into conversation how unfair world is to women, how horrible it is that she was raped, how women should have a right to withdraw consent three months after having sex, how no man should ever hit a woman, not even if she is slicing and dicing his genitals, and for bonus points tell her how she is only girl for you, forever, but that she can sleep with any guy she likes because you would not want to patriarchaly enslave her.

I strongly advise using burner cell and fake name, and never taking this type to your home. Yes, some of them are extremely good looking, but they are also extremely insane and by far most likely type to want to harm you, both physically and online through doxxing you and smearing your reputation.

4. Octomom. MILF. Single mom. Some are just looking for fun. But majority are looking for somebody to be a father to their children. And you will forever be playing second fiddle to their kids. They usually have several children, by multiple men. Those men might, or might not, be still in her life. They might be under the impression that they are getting back together. They might be in prison, and suddenly come back and find you in bed with her.

Her kids might be a minor issue, where she just needs to find a babysitter, or she might have a kid that will make your visit very unpleasant.

To be on the safe side, try to tap Octomoms away from their nests. And away from yours.

5.   Escorts. Prostitutes. They just want your money. I include cam girls here as well, those that will never meet you physically but just want you to pay to see them on a webcam. It's inevitable that you will run into them. Any PM you get that requires you to go register on some site is a sign that you are contacted by a prostitute. Do yourself a favor and cut contact with that person. Odds are that it's a scam.

6.   Attention Whore. This one does look good, but does not intend to ever meet you in person or do anything with you. Odds are that she is in a relationship of some kind and that her guy is not paying her enough attention. Maybe they split up for the night. If she wanted to cheat she would have went out. If you look really good in your pics she might converse with you for a while, just to use you to boost her own self-esteem, but that's about it.

7. Fun Girl. This is what you are looking for. She will be slightly overweight, or butter face. A solid 5 or a 6. Kind of girl that you will want to have sex with but that you would not normally hit on offline because you would be hitting on her better looking friends.

Is that list depressing? Well, it should be. That is a reality of online dating scene. There is some cross-sectioning among those groups. Mostly in that probably majority of girls will have had at least one kid, be overweight somewhat and will at least borderline be attention whoring.

HOW TO READ GIRLS ONLINE DATING PROFILES

When any person writes their online dating profile they want to minimize their negatives. I am going to give you a short list, a dictionary of sorts, a decoder, to be able to quickly ascertain what you are dealing with in reality. These are not listed in any particular order, I merely went through couple hundred profiles and grabbed terms that appear often and then I assessed women using these terms through brief conversation while psychologically profiling them.

BBW means 'Big Beautiful Woman'. Reality is that she might, or might not, have ok face, but fact remains that she will be morbidly obese.

Cuddly means morbidly obese.

Curvy means fat, most likely morbidly obese.

Size X. The X can be any number. If girl feels need to write her dress size you can expect that actual size is at least two to three numbers higher and that 'Size X' is the smallest number she can squish herself into. So might as well read as morbidly obese.

Bubbly. This is fat, flirty and annoying rolled into one. Most likely also pushy and a meddler.

Great Personality means that she is very ugly and that she knows it.

Age X. Add five to ten years to whatever age she listed. If she says she is 35, she is probably 45+. If she says 29, count on her being in mid-30's. If she is younger than 29 it's probably her real age.

Playful. A slut. Slept with more than a hundred guys. It's your turn.

Lives Life To The Fullest. Or just Loves Life. Alcoholic, drug addict and a slut.

Girly means that she is a shallow idiot. She will generalize based on person being male or female.

Adorable means childish, annoying and probably mentally unstable.

Fiery means psychotic. Will probably try to murder you, will definitely scratch your car, and maybe poison your pets.

Vivacious means very aggressive and will physically assault you.

Artistic means drama queen. Most likely has friends around her who are also drama queens. Very likely to post your pictures online and try to humiliate you. Might also call your work and family and say ridiculous things about you in attempt to ruin your life.

Athletic means that she has is flat chested, shapeless and a tomboy. I tend to like this type, as long as they do not want to waste my time by trying to make a date into going to exercise in public. Sexercise is my exercise.

Toned means that she is flat chested, shapeless and a tomboy. I tend to like this type as smaller breasts do not bother me.

Homely means plain and that she wants to nest.

Likes Finer Things In Life. Gold Digger. Prostitute. You can get laid by this one no matter how repulsive you might be as long as you can afford her allowance.

Romantic. She wants to get married quickly. Might be immigrant that needs to marry to stay in the country, or has children, or wants children and is getting close to her 40's.

Challenging. High-maintenance and a pain to deal with.

Loyal. Jealous Stalker. This girl will Google your name faster than you can spell it, access your Facebook when you are not looking, and will refuse to accept it's over. On her Facebook timeline she will be posting about you constantly, and then she will be threatening any girl who you talk to.

Honest. Lacks tact. I actually like this as I value honesty more than I value tact. You might find her being prone to say things that might embarrass you in public too much to handle.

Sensitive. Cries a lot. Stay away unless crying turns you on.

Attractive. It means that she has two eyes, two ears and a mouth. With or without teeth.

Fairly Attractive. It means that she is probably fat, or missing a limb.

Told Attractive. Only by her own mother.

Discretion Expected. 'I'm married and I do not want my wife to know'.

Discretion Offered. 'I do not care if you are married.'

Hope You Like My Picture. It's a 20 year old picture.

Not Just Looking For Sex. Looking Just For Sex. Cunning Reverse Psychology.

Willing To Travel. Lives in a dump which she does not want you to see, or where husband/boyfriend/children always hang out and any other place is probably better.

Adventurous. Kinky and perverted.

Normal. Psycho.

Good Sense Of Humor. NO Sense Of Humor.

Earns A Six-Figure Salary. Includes pennies in that figure, so … it's a Four Figure Salary.

Never done this. Done it a thousand times before but does not want to admit it.

Fun. Childish and/or slutty. I go for this.

Looks Not Important. Can't afford to be a chooser.

Sporty. Fat alcoholic who watches sports all day long and has far too many male 'friends' that she already had sex with.

Unique. Probably was a man and is now a "woman".

Not Into emailing. Boring and desperate. Probably will lay you fast.

Independent. Lying, cheating, commitment-phobic. Perfect for a guilt free quick lay.

Unconventional. Insane. The sort of person you run from over a rush hour highway on foot.

Aspirational. Broke. That means you can hire her as your sex toy for price of a doughnut.

YOUR ONLINE DATING PROFILE

Yeah, you have to make one. And most guys do it all wrong. Lucky for you, I'll tell you how to do this perfectly.

Most important thing to understand is that you should not lie about anything that you might get caught about. It will not only end your game but they will take your pictures and post them on various blogs calling you names. Seriously. You must play a nice guy to a point to avoid severe backlash.

First you need to make sure that you have exactly three perfect pictures.

Your main profile picture only needs to show your face. Do not pretend to be someone else unless you have no intention of ever meeting any of these women in person. There is a lot you can get away with, but unlike women who might get a guy to stick around after he shows up and sees they look different, odds of a man pulling that off are right next to zero.

Make it a recent, month old tops, clean, well lit, head shot. You can wear glasses or shades. If you do, they might ask you to show them picture without, or report your profile pic for not clearly showing your face. I choose to post only face pics wearing shades anyway. It shows that I am attractive but it makes it harder to recognize me. This picture is to let them know what you really look like and what to expect. If there is no physical attraction at all its better if they do not waste more of your time than needed.

Second picture should show you, depending on type of demographic you are going after, either with children/pets (do not need to be your own) in family friendly surrounding or in the club surrounded with girls and maybe party favors. Either way you must look like you are having best time of your life. Purpose of this picture is to make you look like exactly the kind of guy they want to be with. Unlike men who can be happy with just attractiveness, women are more complicated, more psychological. Not all, and not all the time, but, remember, we are playing numbers here. I go with club scene as my profiles tend to be 'party guy'. Not always.

Third, and last, picture should show you engaging in a physical activity. Rock climbing is great here, but almost any kind of physical activity where she can see that you are fully able bodied individual, capable of satisfying her sexual desires, would work. If you are not fully able bodied, I suggest that you select picture that demonstrates as clearly as possible that you lead an active life.

Stop at these three pictures. Resist urge to post more. You want them interested but not feeling like they already know everything there is about you.

Do not have a picture of you posing next to cars that you do not currently own.

Unless you have incredible physique avoid posting shirtless photos. And even then, from my experience, it brings far too much negative attention. Ugly people try to troll you as haters. Instead, wait until she asks for one, then PM it to her.

Do not post pictures of you standing next to better looking guys. There are girls out there that will waste your time and money just to try to meet your friend. You will go on a date, pay for her, and not get laid. Do not be stupid. Unattractive girls can get away with posting pictures of themselves standing next to prettier girls as desperate guys have low self-control. They will still bang willing female. As a guy who's less good looking friends used pics with me in them to attract girls, I am giving you brotherly advice, do not do it. You might lose a friend if you cannot forgive him that he slept with a girl you brought around who never put out for you.

When you write your profile it needs to be short.

More you write, more you risk writing something that will turn her off.

You want to minimize things that will turn her off at a glance.

Simplistic profile might say something like 'Hi, my name is Jack, I am very new to this and little bit shy. My work, while very rewarding and well paying, tends to keep me too busy to go out and meet new people and all the girls I work with are in long term relationships. So, I am just looking to meet some new people, have some fun, and see how things go'.

As interests you put whatever interests you think you might share with some females. And that's it.

Later, if you want, you can refine that profile, based on whatever girls you talk to end up saying. But never convey any feelings in your profile. Under no circumstances do you want girl who might like you to come, read nonsense like 'my marriage just ended and …' or 'I just broke up with my girlfriend …' or 'I hate all women because they are all sluts …' just use bit of common sense. No matter how depressed you might be at any given moment, you must NOT convey that depression. You MUST appear to ALWAYS be having fun. I had to include this paragraph because I just had a conversation with good friend who just refuses to shut up about his ex, and if he's getting on nerves of his guy friends, you can imagine what kind of signals he sends to all the girls who would sleep with him. No girl wants some guy who keeps ranting about his problems. Do not bring up your problems. Just don't do it.

Also, do not fill out questionnaires and optional questions. Those dating quizzes they have. It's far, far better to be unknown than to answer wrong to a question she cares about.

If you want to see what happens when you do not take that advice, go Google this:

"Do you think girls have an obligation to shave their legs?"

It's just one question from OK Cupid, and endless men's lives have been ruined by answering it. Just don't do it.

PRIVATE MESSAGING

Private messages are unlikely to be private. Especially if you upset her. Screenshots will go up everywhere, from her Facebook, to blogs about how horrible men on dating sites are.

For that reason do not use your home phone number, or your main cell phone number. Get separate number just for this, that you can easily change.

Having said that, the best advice I can give any guy when talking to a girl he is interested in is:

GET HER NUMBER ASAP!

Do not open with 'Hi', 'Hello', 'How are you doing', probably 99% of guys do that and you will just blend in.

Do not open with 'You so sexy', 'You are hot', 'Let's have sex', and/or picture of your penis. Even sluts are going to be turned off by that.

Instead make a short template. Something like 'I am messaging you because we have ONE and TWO in common and I think we might have a good time if we went out on a date.' Then quickly look at each girls profile and select whatever you like that she mentioned she likes to do to replace ONE and TWO with.

This is so simple to do, yet it alone will put you in top 1% of guys who message her.

Then you PM at least 100-200 girls profiles.

Expect response rates of 1-2% if you are average looking and up to 10%-25% if you are very good looking. Reason it will never be much better than that is because you can expect at least 50% of those profiles to be abandoned. And even if you are in top 1% of guys who message a girl, she still might simply never even look at your profile if your PM is just one of thousands.

Do not take any of that personally, we are playing a numbers game, you do not need higher than 1% response, you just need to score with one of those that does reply. If 200 PM's was not enough, then just PM more girls. Ideally on several services at once.

If girl replies to you, you want to exchange two or three pointless PM's, stuff she will probably laugh at or agree with, but that will place her in happy mood. What exactly you should say will depend on her profile. If she is student of Psychology, since I am expert on subject, I would ask her what are they covering in her classes right now, and then say something interesting. If she is sports fan, maybe into MMA and last night Gina Carano, or whoever, won, I'd mention it and ask if she saw the fight. Stick to her interests, avoid talking about you.

And then you right away go to:

"What are you doing right now? Sounds boring. Wanna do something much more fun?"

And you want her to give you her phone number and ideally meet you. Not with her friends, or in a club, not next week, but right now, even just for a cup of coffee, just you and her.

You do not want to take her number and then not call right away. It would be stupid waste of time. If you wait just two or three days, some forty other guys might have asked for her number, and called her. Strike while the iron is hot.

Avoid talking to one girl too long. The longer you are talking to a girl more likely you are to say something she does not like. And girls split guys into three categories. Guys they will sleep with (A), guys they might sleep with (B) and guys that have no chance at all to sleep with them (C).

Bad boy type goes to A or C. Nice guys end up in B or C.

But after she sleeps with you, it takes lot more for her to move you to C. If you spend too long in B, you get friendzoned and move to C.

So, no matter what you want from her, if you wish to ever have sex with her, do it right away.

Funny thing is that in literally all books and movies aimed at women, there is this long build up, until she finally sleeps with a guy. And guys go through Hell and back to get laid. But all you need to do is sleep with her in first few hours after meeting her, and you break all that.

CONTACT

Do you ever read a book, and then wish you could say something to the author? Perhaps make a suggestion on how to improve next edition? I read a lot and so I do, often. And it's usually very difficult to really get in touch with the author.

So I'm making that step easy for you folks. E-mail I set up just for few recent projects, including this e-Book:

schadenfreude@saintly.com

THE PATH TO SUCCESS

1. How to Make Money Online ASIN: B00V4H9AR2
2. How to Make Money by Being Politically Incorrect ASIN: B0120OZ47W
3. How to Pick-Up Strippers ASIN: B0129AVIKO
4. How to Pick-Up Girls Online ASIN: B012LA6VN6
5. How to Make Money Gambling ASIN: B012XKEHSU

www.ingramcontent.com/pod-product-compliance
Lightning Source LLC
LaVergne TN
LVHW011737280125
802401LV00009B/620